# A Note From Rick Renner

I am on a personal quest to see a "revival of the Bible" so people can establish their lives on a firm foundation that will stand strong and endure the test as end-time storm winds begin to intensify.

In order to experience a revival of the Bible in your personal life, it is important to take time each day to read, receive, and apply its truths to your life. James tells us that if we will continue in the perfect law of liberty — refusing to be forgetful hearers, but determined to be doers — we will be blessed in our ways. As you watch or listen to the programs in this series and work through this corresponding study guide, I trust you will search the Scriptures and allow the Holy Spirit to help you hear something new from God's Word that applies specifically to your life. I encourage you to be a doer of the Word He reveals to you. Whatever the cost, I assure you — it will be worth it.

> Thy words were found, and I did eat them;
> and thy word was unto me the joy and rejoicing of mine heart:
> for I am called by thy name, O Lord God of hosts.
> — Jeremiah 15:16

Your brother and friend in Jesus Christ,

Rick Renner

*RE-CALCULATING: How To Get Back On Track if You've Messed Up Along the Way*

Copyright © 2022 by Rick Renner
P.O. Box 702040
Tulsa, OK 74170

Published by Rick Renner Ministries
www.renner.org

ISBN 13: 978-1-6675-0021-8

eBook ISBN 13: 978-1-6675-0022-5

# How To Use This Study Guide

This five-lesson study guide corresponds to *"RE-CALCULATING: How To Get Back On Track if You've Messed Up Along the Way" With Rick Renner* (Renner TV). Each lesson in this study guide covers a topic that is addressed during the program series, with questions and references supplied to draw you deeper into your own private study of the Scriptures on this subject.

To derive the most benefit from this study guide, consider the following:

**First,** watch or listen to the program prior to working through the corresponding lesson in this guide. (Programs can also be viewed at **renner.org** by clicking on the Media/Archives links or on our Renner Ministries YouTube channel.)

**Second,** take the time to look up the scriptures included in each lesson. Prayerfully consider their application to your own life.

**Third,** use a journal or notebook to make note of your answers to each lesson's Study Questions and Practical Application challenges.

**Fourth,** invest specific time in prayer and in the Word of God to consult with the Holy Spirit. Write down the scriptures or insights He reveals to you.

**Finally,** take action! Whatever the Lord tells you to do according to His Word, do it.

For added insights on this subject, it is recommended that you obtain Rick Renner's books *The Will of God: The Key to Your Success*. You may also select from Rick's other available resources by placing your order at **renner.org** or by calling 1-800-742-5593.

TOPIC

# Jesus' Example of Trusting the Leadership of the Holy Spirit

## SCRIPTURES

1. **John 16:13** — Howbeit when he, the Spirit of truth, is come, he will guide you into all truth....

2. **Psalm 19:13** — Keep back thy servant also from presumptuous sins; let them not have dominion over me: then shall I be upright, and I shall be innocent from the great transgression.

3. **John 11:1-3,5-15** — Now a certain man was sick, named Lazarus, of Bethany, the town of Mary and her sister Martha. (It was that Mary which anointed the Lord with ointment, and wiped his feet with her hair, whose brother Lazarus was sick.) Therefore his sisters sent unto him, saying, Lord, behold, he whom thou lovest is sick.... Now Jesus loved Martha, and her sister, and Lazarus. When he had heard therefore that he was sick, he abode two days still in the same place where he was. Then after that saith he to his disciples, Let us go into Judaea again. His disciples say unto him, Master, the Jews of late sought to stone thee; and goest thou thither again? Jesus answered, Are there not twelve hours in the day? If any man walk in the day, he stumbleth not, because he seeth the light of this world. But if a man walk in the night, he stumbleth, because there is no light in him. These things said he: and after that he saith unto them, Our friend Lazarus sleepeth; but I go, that I may awake him out of sleep. Then said his disciples, Lord, if he sleep, he shall do well. Howbeit Jesus spake of his death: but they thought that he had spoken of taking of rest in sleep. Then said Jesus unto them plainly, Lazarus is dead. And I am glad for your sakes that I was not there....

## GREEK WORDS

1. "guide" — **ὁδηγός** (*hodegos*): a guide who shows a traveler the safest course through an unknown country; a guide who knows the safest, fastest, and most pleasurable route to take.

2. "sick" — **ἀσθενῶν** (*asthenon*): tense, ailing; a word that generally describes a person who is frail in health; people so physically weak that they were unable to travel; it carries the idea of those who were feeble, fragile, faint, incapacitated, disabled, or simply in such poor health that it would be unthinkable to transport them; shut-ins or homebound

3. "sent" — **ἀποστέλλω** (*apostello*): to send a message by a messenger; to dispatch a message with an urgent message

4. "saying" — **λέγουσαι** (*legousai*): repeatedly saying; repeatedly asserting

5. "Lord" — **Κύριε** (*Kurie*): direct form of **κύριος** (*kurios*), lord, or supreme master

6. "behold" — **ἰδού** (*idou*): bewilderment, shock, amazement, and wonder

7. "lovest" — **φιλέω** (*phileo*): a word that has many different facets, including the ideas of fondness, friendship, or love; it could be used to depict friends, or even to express deep affection; to have an affinity for someone; a cherished friend and companion

8. "now" — **δὲ** (*de*): categorically; emphatically; an exclamation mark

9. "[then indeed] he abode" — **τότε μὲν ἔμεινεν** (*tote men emeinen*): regardless, indeed, he stayed put; regardless, indeed, he did not move; regardless, indeed, he did not budge

10. "two days" — **δύο ἡμέρας** (*duo hemeras*): two full, 24-hour days, at least 48 hours

11. "in the same place" — **ἐν...τόπῳ** (*en topos*): in the same place, in the same geographical location; in the same spot

12. "then after that" — **ἔπειτα μετὰ τοῦτο** (*epeita meta touto*): then precisely after this, referring to two full, 24-hour days or 48 hours

13. "disciples" — **μαθητής** (*mathetes*): pupils; learners; those who were learning from Him

14. "say" — **Λέγουσιν** (*legousin*): saying, saying, and kept on saying

15. "Master" — **Ῥαββί** (*Rabbi*): Great one; master teacher; the One with ultimate authority in their lives

16. "late" — **νῦν** (*nun*): right now, at this very moment

17. "sought" — **ζητέω** (*zeteo*): to seek, to search, or to look very intensively; denotes an intense and thorough searching; to search for thoroughly and exhaustively

18. "to stone" — **λιθάζω** (*lithadzo*): to pelt with stones; to stone to death by crushing the head

19. "goest thou thither" — **ὑπάγεις ἐκεῖ** (*hupageis ekei*): you are being led there; you are being directed to go there

20. "walk" — **περιπατέω** (*peripateo*): to walk around; to live and carry on in one general vicinity

21. "in the day" — **ἐν τῇ ἡμέρᾳ** (*en te hemera*): in the day, referring to 12 hours of daylight

22. "stumbleth not" — **οὐ προσκόπτει** (*ou proskoptei*): does not stumble; does not trip; does not experience an assault or a hit

23. "because" — **ὅτι** (*hoti*): pointing to something significant

24. "light" — **φῶς** (*phos*): light; that which enlightens one's path

25. "but" — **δὲ** (*de*): categorically; emphatically; an exclamation mark

26. "in the night" — **ἐν τῇ νυκτί** (*en te nukti*): in the night, in the hours when there is no light

27. "stumbleth" — **προσκόπτω** (*proskopto*): stumbles; trips; experiences assaults and hits

28. "because" — **ὅτι** (*hoti*): pointing to something significant

29. "death" — **θάνατος** (*thanatos*): here, physical death

30. "plainly" — **παρρησίᾳ** (*parresia*): boldly and unquestionably

31. "dead" — **ἀποθνήσκω** (*apothnesko*): physically dead; in a state of decay

32. "I am glad" — **χαίρω** (*chairo*): I rejoice

33. "for your sakes" — **δι' ὑμᾶς** (*di' humas*): on your account; possibly because it would have turned out badly for the disciples

34. "that I was not there" — **ὅτι οὐκ ἤμην ἐκεῖ** (*hoti ouk emen ekei*): specially that I was not there

## SYNOPSIS

The five lessons in this study on ***RE-CALCULATING: How To Get Back On Track if You've Messed Up Along the Way*** will focus on the following topics:

- Jesus' Example of Trusting the Leadership of the Holy Spirit
- Learning To Listen to the Holy Spirit
- Six Signals To Help You Be Led by the Holy Spirit
- Five Points To Help Keep You On Track
- Practical Help in Re-Calculating To Get Back On Track

**The emphasis of this lesson:**

**The Holy Spirit has been given to us as our internal GPS. As sons and daughters of God, He is guiding us moment by moment into our divine destiny. The first person to really tap into the full use of the Holy Spirit's GPS capabilities was Jesus with His decision to wait two days before going to see Lazarus. It's a perfect example of Him being led by the Spirit.**

One of the greatest advantages of today's technology is the invention of GPS. This Global Positioning System is available on virtually every mobile device, and it has the ability to not only tell you where you are, but also get you to where you need to be. And when you make a wrong turn and are heading in the wrong direction, it helps you recalculate and get back on track.

Spiritually speaking, we have been given a supernatural GPS, and He is called the Holy Spirit. As believers, He lives inside us and He stands ready at every moment of every day to lead and guide us in the way we need to go to reach our God-given destiny. When we mess up and get off track, He will recalculate our route to get us back on track with God's plan. The key is learning to tune our spiritual ears to hear His voice and trust His leading.

# The Holy Spirit Is Your 'Guide'

Jesus said, "Howbeit when he, the Spirit of truth, is come, he will guide you into all truth…" (John 16:13). This is one of the greatest gifts of having the Holy Spirit in our life — He is ready, willing, and able to guide our decisions and our steps if we let Him.

The word "guide" in this verse is the Greek word *hodegos*, and it describes *a guide who shows a traveler the safest course through an unknown country*. This word was used to depict *a tour guide* who knows the safest, fastest, and most pleasurable path to take. The reason this guide knows the best route to take and everything about the journey is because he has already been there.

This word *hodegos* — translated here as "guide" — is the term Jesus used to describe the leadership of the Holy Spirit in our lives. He knows everything that is coming up in your life. If you will listen, He will help you avoid the traps the enemy has set and enable you to enjoy the journey.

In fact, we can avoid getting off track if we will pray *before* we take action. This is what we see David doing in Psalm 19:13. He said, "Keep back thy servant also from presumptuous sins; let them not have dominion over me...." Better to be led by the Spirit from the beginning than to think we know the way on our own and make a mess of things.

## Lazarus Was Jesus' Cherished Friend and He Was Deathly Sick

The first person to really tap into the full use of the Holy Spirit's GPS capabilities was Jesus, and the story of Him receiving news of Lazarus' death is a perfect example of this. The Bible says, "Now a certain man was sick, named Lazarus, of Bethany, the town of Mary and her sister Martha. (It was that Mary which anointed the Lord with ointment, and wiped his feet with her hair, whose brother Lazarus was sick.) Therefore his sisters sent unto him, saying, Lord, behold, he whom thou lovest is sick" (John 11:1-3).

Notice the word "sick," which appears twice in these three verses. It is the Greek word *asthenon*, which in this case means *ailing*. It is a word that generally describes *a person who is frail in health* or *people so physically weak that they were unable to travel*. It carries the idea of *those who are feeble, fragile, faint, incapacitated, disabled, or simply in such poor health that it would be unthinkable to transport them*. Essentially, it depicts one that is a *shut-in* or *homebound*. This was Lazarus' condition. He was so physically weak and incapacitated from sickness that his sisters could not take him to Jesus.

So they sent word to Him of Lazarus' critical condition. The word "sent" in Greek is *apostello*, which means *to send a message by a messenger* or *to dispatch a message with an urgent request*. John 11:3 says that the messenger was "... saying, Lord, behold, he whom thou lovest is sick" (John 11:3). In Greek, the word "saying" is *legousai*, which means *repeatedly saying* or *repeatedly asserting*. Hence, the messenger kept *saying* and *saying* and *saying* to Jesus that Lazarus was *feeble, fragile*, and *in extremely poor health*.

When Mary and Martha called Jesus "Lord," they used the Greek word *Kurie*, which is a direct form of *kurios*, meaning *lord* or *supreme master*. They were recognizing His ultimate or supreme authority over their situation and believed that if Jesus would come, He could speak a word and reverse the curse of sickness that was attacking Lazarus.

We know from John 11:3 that Mary and Martha were totally surprised and caught off guard by their brother's debilitating sickness, because the verse includes the word "behold," which is the Greek word *idou*, describing *bewilderment, shock, amazement, and wonder*. That is why they dispatched an urgent message to Jesus repeatedly saying, "…He whom thou lovest is sick" (John 11:3).

Even the word "lovest" is important. It is a form of the Greek word *phileo*, a word that has many different facets, including the ideas of *fondness, friendship*, or *love*. It could be used to depict *friends* or even to express *deep affection*. Moreover, it carries the idea of *having an affinity for someone* — one considered to be *a cherished friend and companion*. Thus, Mary and Martha were appealing to Jesus and saying, "Lord, the one you deeply love and consider your cherished friend is feeble, frail, incapacitated, and right on the verge of death. But if You'll come, Master, you can take authority over the sickness and command it to leave."

## Jesus Stayed Where He Was Two Days Even After Hearing of Lazarus' Condition

When we come to John 11:5, John writes, "Now Jesus loved Martha, and her sister, and Lazarus." Notice the first word "now." It is the Greek word *de*, which is like an exclamation mark, meaning *categorically* or *emphatically*. It is the equivalent of saying, "Now, categorically and most emphatically, Jesus really loved Martha and her sister and Lazarus."

Then in the very next breath, John says, "When he [Jesus] had heard therefore that he [Lazarus] was sick, he abode two days still in the same place where he was" (John 11:6). At first reading, it seems very strange that Jesus would remain where He was and not immediately come to His friends' aid. In fact, when the Bible says "He abode," the Greek literally says "*then indeed* he abode." A better translation of this portion of Scripture would be, "Regardless, indeed, he stayed put," or "Regardless, indeed, he did not move," or "Regardless, indeed, he did not budge."

John said Jesus didn't move for "two days" — the Greek words *duo hemeras*, meaning *two full, 24-hour days* or *at least 48 hours*. Instead, He stayed put "in the same place," which in Greek is *en topos*, and it means *in the same place, in the same geographical location*, or *in the same spot*. Strangely, even after Jesus received urgent news of Lazarus' serious illness, He didn't budge.

# The Disciples Questioned
# Jesus' Abrupt Decision To Go to Judea

The Scripture goes on to say, "Then after that saith he to his disciples, Let us go into Judaea again" (John 11:7). The phrase "then after that" in Greek is *epeita meta touto*, which means *then precisely after this*, referring to the two full, 24-hour days or 48 hours. What was the reason for the abrupt change? Why did Jesus suddenly decide to go to Judea after purposely waiting two extra days?

The disciples were shocked and perplexed by Jesus' actions. John 11:8 says, "His disciples say unto him, Master, the Jews of late sought to stone thee; and goest thou thither again?" In Greek, the word "disciples" here is *mathetes*, which describes *pupils; learners*; or *those who were learning from Him*. The disciples were called to learn and mimic their Master's every move — not debate with Him regarding His decisions. Nevertheless, they were so disturbed by what Jesus was about to do, they began to question Him.

When the Bible says, "His disciples *say* unto him…," the word "say" is the Greek word *legousin*, which signifies *repeated actions*. That means the disciples kept *saying* and *saying* and *saying* one after the other, "…Master, the Jews of late sought to stone thee; and goest thou thither again?" (John 11:8). The word "Master" here is the Greek word *Rabbi*, meaning *Great one; master teacher*; or *the One with ultimate authority in their lives*. This was a title of honor only given to individuals who had a supreme mastery of the Word of God.

Jesus' disciples were respectfully but repeatedly reminding Him that "the Jews of late sought to stone Him." The word "late" here is a translation of the Greek word *nun*, meaning *right now, at this very moment*, and the word "sought" is a form of the Greek word *zeteo*, which means *to seek, to search*, or *to look very intensively*. It denotes *an intense and thorough searching*. The Jewish leaders were *thoroughly* and *exhaustively* combing the country trying to locate Jesus.

Once they found Him, their intentions were *to stone* Him. In Greek, the phrase "to stone" is *lithadzo*, which means *to pelt with stones* or *to stone to death by crushing the head*. Knowing full well what the Jewish leaders were scheming, the disciples questioned Jesus, "Goest thou thither," which in Greek literally means, *"You are being led there, Jesus? You are being directed to go there?"*

# Those Who Live in the Light
# Do Not Stumble

Indeed, Jesus was being led by the Holy Spirit to go to Judea to the town of Bethany where Lazarus and his sisters lived, which is why the Bible says, "Jesus answered, Are there not twelve hours in the day? If any man walk in the day, he stumbleth not, because he seeth the light of this world" (John 11:9). Although this verse may seem unusual, what Jesus is talking about here is being led by the Holy Spirit.

First, notice He says, "…If any man walk in the day…" (John 11:9). The word "walk" here is *peripateo*, which means *to walk around* or *stroll* and carries the idea of *living and carrying on in one general vicinity*. Next, notice the phrase "in the day." It is a translation of the Greek words *en te hemera*, meaning *in the day*, referring to *12 hours of daylight*.

Jesus said, "…If any man walk in the day, he stumbleth not…" (John 11:9). In Greek, the words "stumbleth not" are *ou proskoptei*, and it means *does not stumble; does not trip; does not experience an assault or a hit*. Why is someone walking in the daylight immune to tripping and being assaulted? The reason is "…Because he seeth the light of this world" (John 11:9). The word "because" is the Greek word *hoti*, which is a term *pointing to something significant*. In this case, it points specifically to seeing the "light" of this world. This word "light" is the Greek word *phos*, and it signifies *light* or *that which enlightens one's path*.

# Those Who Live *Without* the Light
# Stumble and Are Susceptible To Assault

In contrast, Jesus went on to say, "But if a man walk in the night, he stumbleth, because there is no light in him" (John 11:10). The word "but" here is the Greek word *de*, which we saw translated as the word "now" in verse 5, and it means *categorically* or *emphatically*. Jesus used this word as an exclamation point to draw attention to the consequences of *not* walking in the light.

He said that if a man walks, which means *to live* or *carry out one's life*, "…in the night, he stumbeleth…" (John 11:10). The phrase "in the night" is a translation of the Greek words *en te nukti*, which means *in the night* or *in the hours when there is no light*. And the Greek word for "stumbleth" is *proskopto*, and it depicts *one stumbling* or *tripping; one who experiences assaults and hits.*

Jesus stated the reason a person stumbles, trips, or is assaulted is "…because there is no light in him" (John 11:10). Again, this word "because" is the word *hoti*, which *points to something significant*, and that is "…there is no light in Him (John 11:10). Remember, Jesus said the Holy Spirit is our guide (*see* John 16:13), and if we will listen to Him, He will provide the light we need to be able to see where we're going and not stumble or be tripped up in life.

In the context of John 11, Jesus didn't budge for two days because the Holy Spirit had not led Him to go. The "light" that the Spirit had given Jesus was to stay put. Once those two days were completed, the Holy Spirit suddenly led Jesus to go, which is why the disciples questioned Him, "Goest thou thither," which in Greek literally means, *"You are being led there, Jesus? You are being directed to go there?"*

## The Holy Spirit Led Jesus To Wait and His Obedience Averted Catastrophe

After explaining the difference between walking in the light and walking in the night, the Bible says, "These things said he: and after that he saith unto them, Our friend Lazarus sleepeth; but I go, that I may awake him out of sleep. Then said his disciples, Lord, if he sleep, he shall do well. Howbeit Jesus spake of his death: but they thought that he had spoken of taking of rest in sleep" (John 11:11-13). The word "death" here is the Greek word *thanatos*, and it describes *physical death*.

Knowing the disciples didn't grasp what He was saying, "Then said Jesus unto them plainly, Lazarus is dead" (John 11:14). The word "plainly" in Greek is *parresia*, meaning *boldly* and *unquestionably*, and the word "dead" is the Greek word *apothnesko*, which means *physically dead* or *in a state of decay*. The Lord let His disciples know in the clearest of terms that Lazarus was dead and already decaying.

To this Jesus added, "And I am glad for your sakes that I was not there…" (John 11:15). The phrase "I am glad" is a translation of the Greek word *chairo*, and it is the equivalent of Him saying, *"I rejoice"* or *"I am thrilled."* This brings us to the phrase "for your sakes," which is *di' humas* in Greek, and it means *on your account*. The implication here is that if Jesus had gone immediately to Bethany to help Lazarus, it possibly would have turned out badly for the disciples.

Again, Jesus said, "And I am glad for your sakes that I was not there..." (John 11:15). The phrase "that I was not there" in Greek is *hoti ouk emen ekei*, and it means *emphatically* or *specially that I was not there*.

It appears that the Jews thought Jesus would come immediately to see Lazarus, and when He arrived, their intention was to stone Him to death and probably to do something horrible to His disciples at the same time. But Jesus didn't show up because the Holy Spirit told Him to stay put.

Naturally speaking, Jesus was very likely moved in His emotions to go see Lazarus the moment He heard he was on the verge of death. Nevertheless, He didn't budge for two days. He waited until He received fresh light from the Holy Spirit and felt a release in His heart to go.

Friend, if you'll listen to the Holy Spirit, He will enlighten your path, telling you when to stay put, when to move, and where you are to go. Begin to listen for the voice of the Holy Spirit and look for His light to guide you every step of the way. What He did for Jesus He will do for you.

## STUDY QUESTIONS

**Study to shew thyself approved unto God, a workman that needeth not to be ashamed, rightly dividing the word of truth.**
**— 2 Timothy 2:15**

1. Prior to this lesson, what did you know about Jesus' relationship with Mary, Martha, and Lazarus? What did you understand the reason was for Jesus waiting two days and not going to see Lazarus immediately? How has this teaching reshaped your perspective?

2. In your own words, describe what Jesus means when He said, "...If any man walk in the day, he stumbleth not, because he seeth the light of this world. But if a man walk in the night, he stumbleth, because there is no light in him (John 11:9,10)?

3. By the time Jesus showed up, Lazarus had been dead for four days and was decaying. Although the situation certainly looked hopeless, how did God supernaturally move in this situation? (*See* John 11:38-45.) What does this say to you about the situations you're currently facing?

## PRACTICAL APPLICATION

**But be ye doers of the word, and not hearers only,
deceiving your own selves.
—James 1:22**

1. Have you ever been in a heart-wrenching situation where you desperately prayed for God's help, and for some reason His help seemed to be delayed? If so, briefly describe what took place.

2. How does knowing that Jesus was led by the Holy Spirit to wait two days before going to Lazarus help you see your situation with new vision?

3. When Mary and Martha called Jesus "Lord," they used the Greek word *Kurie*, which means *lord* or *supreme master*. They recognized Him as the ultimate or supreme authority over their situation. What difficult situation (or situations) are you walking through that you need to recognize Jesus as *supreme master* over? Take time to declare Him as Lord over these things and invite His resurrection power to be displayed for His glory.

## LESSON 2

## TOPIC

# Learning To Listen to the Holy Spirit

## SCRIPTURES

1. **Romans 8:14** — For as many as are led by the Spirit of God, they are the sons of God.

2. **Psalm 19:13** — Keep back thy servant also from presumptuous sins; let them not have dominion over me: then shall I be upright, and I shall be innocent from the great transgression.

## GREEK WORDS

1. "led" — ἄγω (*ago*): to lead: often depicted animals led by a rope tied around their necks, who followed wherever their owner led them; thus to be led; the owner would "tug" and "pull" and the animal followed;

to be led by a gentle tug or pull; this word forms the root for the Greek word ἀγών (*agon*), which describes an intense conflict, such as a struggle in a wrestling match or a struggle of the human will

## SYNOPSIS

Can you imagine 30 million people all making their way into one city at the same time? That's the picture of the morning commute every day in Moscow, Russia. Cars, buses, and rail cars filled with people all converging into one region. Thank goodness for GPS. In addition to helping us find the fastest route, it also notifies us of accidents that we can avoid.

In the same way, the Holy Spirit is our internal GPS that guides our lives. Romans 8:14 says, "For as many as are led by the Spirit of God, they are the sons of God." If we will learn to recognize and listen to the leading of the Holy Spirit, we can avoid many of the accidents that others run into. And even if we have made mistakes and gotten derailed from our destiny, the Spirit will recalculate our route and get us back on track if we'll listen and obey Him.

**The emphasis of this lesson:**

**The Holy Spirit is the Spirit of Truth, which means He can be fully trusted. Usually when He is leading us, He gently tugs or pulls on our heart, giving an inner nudge to do or not do something. When the Spirit is leading us in a certain direction, our job is to follow and obediently stay where He guides us — even if it makes no sense to our mind.**

## The Holy Spirit Is the Greatest Tour Guide

Just hours before being brutally beaten and crucified on the Cross, Jesus spoke candidly with His disciples, giving them vital information they would need to carry on once He was gone. John records His final words in great detail, and in chapters 14, 15, and 16, he captures what Jesus had to say about the ministry of the Holy Spirit. Three times in these three chapters, Jesus calls the Holy Spirit the *Spirit of Truth*. He is *not* called the Spirit of error, the Spirit of deception, or the Spirit of dishonesty. He is the Spirit of Truth, which lets us know that He can be fully trusted.

In John 16:13, Jesus declared, "Howbeit when he, the Spirit of truth, is come, he will guide you into all truth…." We saw that the word "guide" in Greek is the word *hodegos*, which is taken from the word *hodas*, the term for a *road*. When *hodas* becomes *hodegos*, it describes *one who knows all the roads*. It is the Greek word for a *tour guide* — *one who shows a traveler the safest course through an unknown country*. Thus, the Holy Spirit is a guide who knows the safest, fastest, and most pleasurable route to take.

It is no accident that Jesus chose the word *hodegos* (guide) to describe the work of the Holy Spirit. He is the greatest tour guide you will ever have because He has already been to your future and has seen what lies ahead for you. He knows all the roads and the best routes to take and the ones you need to avoid. Instead of trying to figure out where you should go and how you should get there, God wants you to listen to the voice of His Spirit and allow Him to lead you safely and expediently where you need to go. He will take you on the most exciting, most enjoyable journey ever.

Many times we get off track and get into trouble because we presume that we know what God wants us to do. David certainly experienced his fair share of self-induced disasters that took control of his life, which is why he prayed, "Keep back thy servant also from presumptuous sins; let them not have dominion over me: then shall I be upright, and I shall be innocent from the great transgression" (Psalm 19:13). If we will learn to cry out to God for His direction *first*, we can avoid the messes that take place when we lean to our own understanding.

## What Does It Mean To Be 'Led' by the Spirit?

Looking once more at Romans 8:14, it says, "For as many as are led by the Spirit of God, they are the sons of God." The word "led" here is very important. It is a form of the Greek word *ago*, which means *to lead*. What's interesting about this word is that it is an agricultural term that often depicted animals being led by a rope tied around their necks, following wherever their owner led them. Thus, to be led, the owner would "tug" and "pull" on the rope, and the animal obediently followed.

A perfect example of this is the elderly woman who lived near Rick and Denise's farmhouse when they first moved to the former Soviet Union. Since she didn't have much grass on her property, she would wrap a rope around the neck of her cow every morning, lead it to the Renner's front yard, and then tie the rope to the end of a stake she hammered into the ground. She'd then slap her cow on the side and say, "See you later," and go home. The cow would stay put where it had been led.

Amazingly, that huge cow, weighing nearly 1,500 pounds, obediently followed that little woman and then stayed where it was led. As big and strong as the cow was, it could have easily knocked the woman flat or pulled the stake out of the ground and run off, but it never did. When Rick asked one of the local townspeople about the cow and why it listened to the little lady, they said, "It's simple. The cow follows its owner and stays where it is led because it was trained to follow since the time it was young and began to walk." That is what this word *ago* pictures: being led by a gentle tug or pull.

Again, the Bible says, "For as many as are led by the Spirit of God, they are the sons of God." The Holy Spirit is like the owner who leads us to green pastures to be fed and to rest. He's out in front, and we're tagging along behind Him. In most cases, the Spirit's leading is a gentle tug or pull on our heart strings — an inner nudge or sensation to do or not do something. When the Spirit is gently leading us in a certain direction, our job is to follow and then obediently stay where He leads us. Remember, He is the Spirit of Truth that can be fully trusted.

## Rick Learned a Powerful Lesson ...the Hard Way

Now there's something else you need to know about this word *ago*, which is translated here as "led." It forms the root for the Greek word *agon*, which describes *an intense conflict*, such as the struggle in a wrestling match, only in this case it is *the struggle of the human will*. This tells us that sometimes when the Holy Spirit tries to lead us, our heart senses that He is directing our steps and says yes to His leadership. Our mind, however, doesn't understand and begins to reason and wrangle against it.

Rick shared this personal story from the pages of his life that perfectly illustrates just how important it is to listen to and obey the promptings of the Holy Spirit when you sense He is leading you:

Many years ago, Denise and I were ministering at a big conference in Chicago, and since we were living in the former Soviet Union, seeing our friends in the States was very exciting. One day, after speaking in the morning session, we returned to our hotel where we laid down to get some rest before we went to the evening service. As I lay on the bed, I began to be deeply disturbed inside. For some reason, I sensed I wasn't supposed to leave the hotel room that night. But in my mind, I thought, *Why would the*

*Holy Spirit want me to stay in this room when I could go to the meeting and receive wonderful ministry — and see our friends?*

As we got up and got dressed, I said to Denise, "I don't know why, but I feel the Holy Spirit tugging on my heart, urging me not to leave this room tonight. I don't know why He would tell me to do that?" And Denise responded, "Well Rick, you better do whatever you feel He is impressing you to do."

In that moment, a war — an *agon* or *struggle of my human will* — began to rage. Although I sensed in my heart I was to stay put in the room, my head kept saying, *Why in the world would God want me to remain in this room by myself?* After going back and forth between these two ideas, I finally convinced myself that the thoughts to stay in the room were sheer nonsense. *This must be my imagination,* I thought. So I overrode the uneasiness in my spirit and made the decision to go to the meeting.

Just before leaving the hotel, there was a gentle knock at our door. "Just a minute," I said. But by the time I got to the door and opened it, there was no one there. As strange as it seemed, I quickly dismissed it and went downstairs with Denise to get into the car and head back to the evening meeting on the other side of the city.

The entire time Denise and I were in route to the church, I was grieved and weighed down on the inside. Several times I turned to Denise and said, "I don't know why, but I feel like this car needs to turn around and take me back to the hotel room. For some reason, I'm supposed to be in that room tonight." Again, Denise responded, "Rick, you better do whatever you feel impressed to do."

Then just as I was about to ask the driver to take me back to the hotel, my mind would kick in and reason it away, saying, *Nah, that doesn't make any sense. Why would God want me to sit in a room by myself when I could be in a great meeting receiving wonderful ministry?* Back and forth I went, again and again. *Go back to the hotel and stay in the room or go to the meeting. What should I do?* I thought.

At one point, even the driver got involved in our conversation. "I can certainly take you back to the hotel, Mr. Renner. Just say the word and I'll turn around." At that point, I was kind of embarrassed because of my doublemindedness.

"No, it's okay," I said. "We're going to go to the meeting."

Finally, we made it to the church where we greeted our friends with handshakes and hugs and enjoyed some light conversation over coffee. But just as we all turned to walk into the auditorium for the meeting, the intensity of the inward grief became even stronger. In that moment, I said, "Denise, I don't know what's going on, but for some reason I feel like I'm being pulled back to our hotel room tonight. It doesn't make any sense, but it seems like the Holy Spirit is telling me to go back to the room and get there as fast as I can. I can't go into the service." After quickly kissing Denise goodbye and waving to our friends, I reconnected with our driver and asked him to take me back to our hotel.

As we made our way back across town, I suddenly realized I was going to miss dinner, so I asked the driver to pull into a fast-food restaurant so I could get something to eat. Once I had my burger and fries, I remembered I needed toothpaste. Ironically, there just happened to be a convenience store a few feet away, so I went inside and took my time strolling up and down the aisles. Finally, after I bought the toothpaste, I made my way back to the car.

When I got back to the hotel and walked into the lobby, the desk clerk said, "Why are you back from the meeting so early? Isn't it still going on?" Rather than try to explain to her about feeling led to return to the hotel and be in my room, I chose to visit with her for a little while. Eventually, I made my way to the elevator and back up to our room.

At that point, a great deal of time had passed. When I finally reached our door, I noticed that it was cracked open. Pushing it back, I walked into the room, and it looked as though a hurricane had blown through. Our suitcases were open, and our clothes were thrown around everywhere. Immediately, I noticed Denise's jewelry box had been tossed to the floor, and it was empty. Nothing left but some cheap costume jewelry scattered around.

Frantic, I turned and looked over at the desk where I had left my computer and my briefcase. Both were now gone. Of all our possessions, these were most important. My briefcase contained my passport and all of our legal documents, and on my computer were five unpublished books that I was writing — and I had no additional copies.

As I stood there in a state of shock and gazed around the room, it took me a few seconds to realize we had been robbed. Someone had come in after we had left and ransacked the room. They had gone through all our luggage and stolen my briefcase, my computer, and all of Denise's beautiful jewelry — some of which was brand new. Everything of value was taken, and I felt so violated.

Instantly, I heard the still, small voice of the Holy Spirit say, "Now you know why I was leading you to stay in the room tonight." Wow! I learned a valuable lesson from that experience: Always listen to and obey the guiding voice of the Holy Spirit, and catastrophes like these can be avoided.

## Choose To Obey the Spirit's Leading and Turn a Deaf Ear to Mental Reasoning

Friend, the Holy Spirit is your personal tour guide, which means He has already been to and seen your future. He knows everything that's going to happen up ahead and what the enemy is going to try to do to steal, kill, and destroy the good things God has planned. If you will listen to Him, He will lead and guide you to the right place at the right time.

Like Rick, there will be times when the Holy Spirit is leading you in your heart, but it won't make sense to your mind. In those moments, you must choose to obey His gentle tug and turn a deaf ear to the reasoning in your mind. Think about it. The Holy Spirit knew that someone was going to break into Rick and Denise's room that night. Had Rick listened to the gut feeling of the Holy Spirit and stayed in the room, nothing would have happened.

In fact, that is what happens sometimes. We sense we are to be in a certain place or do something specific, and after we do what we feel God is asking us to do, nothing seems to come of it. When it's over, we often say to ourselves, *I thought for sure the Holy Spirit was leading me to do this, but I don't see why. Nothing happened. I guess I must have missed Him.*

The truth is your obedience may very well have stopped something significant from happening that the enemy had planned against you. Only eternity will tell for sure what you avoided by listening to the leading of the Spirit. So just because "nothing happened" doesn't mean you missed God's leading. It may be that you were totally in sync with the Holy Spirit.

## STUDY QUESTIONS

**Study to shew thyself approved unto God, a workman that
needeth not to be ashamed, rightly dividing the word of truth.**
**— 2 Timothy 2:15**

1. According to Isaiah 55:12 and Colossians 3:15, what is the most common impression the Holy Spirit gives us in our heart to let us know He is leading us to do something? How would you describe the absence of this feeling and what would it indicate the Holy Spirit is saying?

2. Imagine a friend you've been praying for a long time just got saved and has made Jesus Lord of their life. Taking what you're learning about the Holy Spirit, what would you tell them about the Spirit being their "tour guide"? How would you explain what it means to be "led by the Spirit"?

## PRACTICAL APPLICATION

**But be ye doers of the word, and not hearers only,
deceiving your own selves.**
**— James 1:22**

1. Usually the leading of the Holy Spirit is *a gentle tug or pull.* Can you remember a time when you sensed the Spirit gently directing you to do or not do something? What was it? Did you obey His leading? What was the outcome of your actions and what did you learn from the situation?

2. There are also times when the Holy Spirit's leading is like a wrestling match where our human will struggles to obey what He's asking us to do. Can you recall a situation like this? If so, what was the Holy Spirit prompting you to do? Did you obey Him? If you didn't, *why?* If you had the chance to go back and relive those moments, what would you change?

3. Be honest: Has the Holy Spirit been trying to guide you in a specific area, and you haven't listened to Him? What has He been asking you to do — or *not* do? How has this lesson put a reverential fear of God in you to repent for your inaction and begin obeying the Spirit's leading?

TOPIC

# Six Signals To Help You Be Led by the Holy Spirit

## SCRIPTURES

1. **Psalm 73:24** — Thou shalt guide me with thy counsel, and afterward receive me to glory.

2. **Psalm 19:13** — Keep back thy servant also from presumptuous sins; let them not have dominion over me: then shall I be upright, and I shall be innocent from the great transgression.

3. **2 Corinthians 13:1** — …In the mouth of two or three witnesses shall every word be established.

4. **1 John 5:14,15** — And this is the confidence that we have in him, that, if we ask any thing according to his will [the Bible], he heareth us: And if we know that he hear us, whatsoever we ask, we know that we have the petitions that we desired of him.

5. **Romans 8:14** —For as many as are led by the Spirit of God, they are the sons of God.

6. **Psalm 37:4** — Delight thyself also in the Lord: and he shall give thee the desires of thine heart.

7. **Psalm 20:4** (*NLT*) — May he grant your heart's desires and make all your plans succeed.

8. **Romans 14:23** — …Whatsoever is not of faith is sin.

9. **Hebrews 10:7** (*NLT*) — Then I said, 'Look, I have come to do Your will, O God — as it is written about me in the Scriptures.'

10. **Hebrews 11:6** — But without faith it is impossible to please him [God]….

## GREEK WORDS

There are no Greek words in this lesson.

## SYNOPSIS

As we have seen in our previous lessons, the Holy Spirit serves as our internal GPS, ready to lead and guide us in every situation and through every decision. His supernatural presence and power in our life are always on the cutting edge and never need an upgrade! If we'll listen to His voice, He will show us what roads to take and which ones to avoid, and if we make a mistake along the way, He will recalculate our position and tell us what we need to do to get back on track.

If you're listening to and trusting the GPS on your phone, how much more should you be listening to and trusting the voice of the Holy Spirit who is guiding your life? Psalm 73:24 says, "Thou shalt guide me with thy counsel, and afterward receive me to glory." It is God's promise to lead you in this life and then take you into Heaven to be with Him for eternity. How can we know the Spirit of God is leading us? There are six common markers that confirm His voice.

**The emphasis of this lesson:**

**The six signals that confirm you are indeed being led by the Holy Spirit are: (1) the voice of God's Word; (2) the voice of the Holy Spirit; (3) the voice of your own heart; (4) the voice of spiritual leaders; (5) the voice of circumstances; and (6) the voice of faith.**

# A Review of Lessons 1 and 2

In **Lesson 1**, we examined Jesus' words in John 16:13 where He says, "Howbeit when he, the Spirit of truth, is come, he will guide you into all truth...." We saw that the word "guide" is the Greek word *hodegos*, which describes *one who knows all the roads*. It is the Greek term for a *tour guide — one who shows a traveler the safest course through an unknown country.* Hence, the Holy Spirit is a guide who knows the safest, fastest, and most pleasurable route to take. Jesus Himself relied on the leading of the Holy Spirit all throughout His own life.

In **Lesson 2**, we looked at Paul's words in Romans 8:14, which says, "For as many as are led by the Spirit of God, they are the sons of God." This means that if you are God's child, you have a right to be led — and should expect to be led — by the Holy Spirit. Unfortunately, many of us make the mistake of acting presumptuously — thinking we know what's best for us and what direction we should go in. To counteract this tendency, we should pray like David prayed, "Keep back thy servant also from presumptuous sins; let them not have dominion over me: then shall I be upright, and I shall be innocent from the great transgression" (Psalm 19:13).

[If you want to know more about being led by God's Spirit and abiding in His will, we recommend Rick's series *Knowing the Will of God*. You can obtain this resource online at **renner.org** or by calling 1-800-742-5593.

# Truth Is Established in the Mouth of Two or Three Witnesses

How can you know for sure that what you're hearing and sensing in your spirit is indeed the Spirit of Truth speaking to you? Under the inspiration of the Holy Spirit, the apostle Paul gave us this reliable litmus test: "…In the mouth of two or three witnesses shall every word be established" (2 Corinthians 13:1).

This verse says when God is leading, He confirms it in the mouth of multiple "witnesses." He may confirm it through the mouth of your pastor, through the words of a trusted friend, or through a circumstance. Likewise, you may be reading the Bible and suddenly a verse speaks to your heart. When God does that, it gives you a very firm foundation for you to stand on.

When there are multiple witnesses confirming something in your life, it is like a *green light* signaling you to move forward. If there are conflicting signs, it is like a *yellow light* of caution telling you to slow down. And if you see several signals that seem to say, "No, don't do this," you need to take it as a *red light* and proceed no further. Here is a more detailed look at six specific, biblical witnesses that God uses regularly to speak to us:

## WITNESS #1: The Voice of the Bible

The first and foremost witness God gives us to confirm His leading in our life is *the voice of the Bible*. The God who is leading you is the same God who inspired the Bible, and He will never lead you to do something contradictory to what He has clearly stated in His Word. Anything that goes against what is taught in the Bible will never be the will of God.

For example, *adultery* is never the will of God. When people want an adulterous relationship, they often begin to rationalize and justify their actions. They think, *Maybe God is creating this new relationship to make up for the emotional deficit I've had in my life.* But that kind of reasoning is devilish deception, because God is against adultery and would never lead a person into an adulteress relationship.

Likewise, *stealing* is never the will of God. The Bible clearly says not to steal (*see* Exodus 20:15), so you don't even need to pray about that. God would never lead you to steal. Similarly, *lying* is never the will of God and neither is being *disrespectful to authority*. Although we may think that because someone in leadership is mistreating those under them it is okay to be disrespectful, it is not.

You cannot excuse behaviors like these or even convince yourself that maybe, somehow, in some way, in this particular case, God is making an exception. That's not how He does things. If He has already spoken something in His Word, He is not going to lead you to go against it. Again, the God who inspired the Bible will never lead you to do something that is contradictory to its teachings.

First John 5:14 and 15 says, "And this is the confidence that we have in him, that, if we ask any thing according to his will [that's the Bible], he heareth us; And if we know that he hear us, whatsoever we ask, we know that we have the petitions that we desired of him." When we stick with the Bible, we are on safe ground because the Bible reveals the will of God.

For instance, healing is the will of God because it is found in the Bible. Walking in integrity and tithing are also the will of God as they, too, are promoted in the pages of Scripture. Any issue that is clearly addressed in God's Word, you don't have to pray about. If He authorizes it in His Word, you can do it. If God is against it in His Word, He will not lead you to do it. The God who is leading you is the same God who inspired the Bible, and He will not lead you to do things contradictory to what He has stated in His Word.

God's revealed will is found in His Word. That is why it is so important for you to read the Bible. If you don't have a daily reading guide, contact Renner Ministries, and we will help you get one.

## WITNESS #2: The Voice of the Holy Spirit

The second witness God has given us to confirm His leading in our life is *the voice of the Holy Spirit*. If we will listen, the Holy Spirit will lead us.

That is what we learned in Lesson 2. The Bible says, "As many as are led by the Spirit of God, they are the sons of God" (Romans 8:14).

This means if we are children of God, we have a right to be *led* by the Holy Spirit. Remember, the word "led" is the Greek word *ago*, which is an agricultural term that was often used to depict animals led by a rope tied around their necks. By a simple tug or gentle pull, the animal obediently followed wherever their owner led them. This is a picture of the Holy Spirit leading us.

Interestingly, the original Greek text of Romans 8:14 actually says, "As many as by the Spirit of God are being led, they are the sons of God." This positions the Holy Spirit out in front and us tagging along behind Him. He usually doesn't lead us by thunderbolts or angelic appearances. Instead, He gently tugs on our hearts, pulling us into the direction of His will.

Jesus referred to the Holy Spirit as the Spirit of Truth three times in John 14, 15, and 16. He is not called the Spirit of error, the Spirit of deception, or the Spirit of dishonesty. He is the Spirit of Truth who can be totally trusted. When you sense Him leading you in your heart but don't understand it in your head, reject the reasoning of your mind and choose to listen to what He's saying. He has your best interest at heart and will never lead you astray.

## Witness #3: The Voice of Your Own Heart

The third witness God often uses to confirm His leading is *the voice of your own heart*. Psalm 37:4 says, "Delight thyself also in the Lord: and he shall give thee the desires of thine heart." As you live in relationship with Him, He will give you the desires of your heart. Although, He will never give you desires that are contrary to the teaching of Scripture, He Himself will put the right desires in your heart that are in harmony with His will for your life.

Many times we're struggling to know if we're really being led by God, but if we will just listen to our hearts, we will know whether or not we're headed in the right direction. For instance, if your heart is crying out to sing or to teach, and you're constantly praying, "God, please show me your will," it is probably Him giving you a desire to sing or teach. Likewise, if your heart is burning to be in business, it may be that God has put the desire for business inside your heart.

If you are wanting to do God's will and praying for Him to show you what it is, it is probably already exploding in your heart. Your heart has a voice, and it's speaking to you. If you'll listen, it will confirm the direction He wants you to go in. As Psalm 20:4 (*NLT*) says, "May he grant your heart's desires and make all your plans succeed."

## WITNESS #4: The Voice of Spiritual Leaders

The fourth witness God often uses to direct our lives is *the voice of spiritual leaders*. Older, more mature believers who know us well can help us discern the will of God for our life. But in order to benefit from the unbiased wisdom, we have to be open to hear what they have to say.

Rick shared an example of how when he and Denise were first married, he wanted to purchase an old house in the city where they lived. It was a relic from the Civil War era, and it was so dilapidated that at one time some filmmakers had set it on fire and used the footage in a movie. Rick had always had a desire to renovate homes or to upgrade property, so he began the process of purchasing the old house and working to get it renovated.

From the beginning, there were a number of red flags regarding the venture — the first being he and Denise were not in unity on purchasing the house. The second obvious reason was that they didn't have the money to do the needed renovations. Yet, regardless of these warning signs and the fact that the house was in a heap of ruins, Rick continued to move forward with attempting to purchase it.

Then one day when he was at the house trying to shovel a foot of bird manure off the attic floor, an older, seasoned leader from the church stopped by to offer some words of wisdom. "Rick," he said politely, "what in the world are you doing? Let's take a moment and really walk through this. Would God lead you to do a project like this when you don't have the money for it? If He were leading you to take on this task, wouldn't He provide you the resources? You may start the renovations, but you won't be able to finish them, which is going to become a real problem."

At first, Rick admitted he was very offended because he thought the older man just didn't have any vision or faith for the project. But after he pointed out the pitfalls, God enabled Rick to understand that he was just excited about having a project, and it just wasn't wise or practical for him to do at that season in his life. God used this older, seasoned leader to show Rick he was not being led by the Holy Spirit. His words of wisdom were effective because Rick was willing to listen and submit to what this wise man said.

Just as we need to listen to the voice of the Bible, the voice of the Holy Spirit, and the voice of our own heart, we also need to listen to the voice of older, mature spiritual leaders who speak into our lives. Very often they can see things more clearly than we can. That may be your parent, your pastor, a person who is discipling you, or someone older than you in the Lord. Whatever the case may be, keep your ears open and your heart receptive to what seasoned leaders speak into your life. They very well may be one of the two or three witnesses God uses to lead you and possibly spare you from making a disastrous mistake.

## Witness #5: The Voice of Circumstances

The fifth witness God often uses to establish what He is speaking to us is *the voice of circumstances*. Of all the ways God directs us, this is the lowest level. Nevertheless, while you should not be led by circumstances alone, you should also not ignore them.

Very often, when things line up, it is a "green light" or a confirmation that you are supposed to do something. Likewise, when doors slam shut, it is often a signal that you are headed in the wrong direction. Many times, one or more doors will close before the right door opens, so don't be discouraged by a door that closes. It may be that God is saving you from heartache and preparing you for an opportunity you never dreamed was possible.

So pay attention to circumstances, but don't be led by circumstances alone. Let them speak alongside the witness of God's Word, the Holy Spirit, your heart, and the wisdom of seasoned leaders.

## Witness #6: The Voice of Faith

The sixth and final witness we want to briefly look at is *the voice of faith*. Will the endeavor you feel you are being led by God to do require faith to accomplish it? The Bible says, "…Whatsoever is not of faith is sin" (Romans 14:23).

Oftentimes when God is leading you to do something, it will usually require an increase in your faith. If it is a true leading of the Lord, it means your faith will be challenged, your faith will be stretched, and you will be required to grow.

God is not only interested in just using us — He wants to *transform* us and *mature* us in the process. He wants us to go from strength to strength and grow from glory to glory. Thus, when God asks you to do something, it will require faith.

Think about Moses. When he led the children of Israel through the Red Sea, it required faith. In the same way, when God told Joshua to lead the children of Israel across the Jordan River into the land of promise, they had to cross the Jordan at flood stage, which also required faith.

And what about Jesus? For Him to come into the world to redeem us, it required faith. Jesus said, "...Look, I have come to do Your will, O God — as it is written about me in the Scriptures" (Hebrews 10:7 *NLT*). God's will for Jesus was to be born as a baby, to minister as a man, to die on the Cross, and then descend into hell for three days. All the while He was to trust that the Father would raise Him from the dead. Therefore, every step of Jesus' life required faith.

Indeed, as the Bible declares, "But without faith it is impossible to please Him [God]..." (Hebrews 11:6). Whatever the Holy Spirit is leading you to do will require faith.

## You Can Be Confident That God Will Always Confirm His Leading

Friend, when you are seeking God's will in any area of your life, He will use a combination of these six voices to speak to you and confirm if you are aligned with His will or not. Once again these voices include:

1. **The voice of God's Word.**
2. **The voice of the Holy Spirit.**
3. **The voice of your own heart.**
4. **The voice of spiritual leaders.**
5. **The voice of circumstances.**
6. **The voice of faith.**

Remember, God said, "...In the mouth of two or three witnesses shall every word be established" (2 Corinthians 13:1). If all of these "witnesses" say yes, you have a "green light" — a confirmation from God to move forward with His blessing. If several of these voices say "no," you need to proceed with caution. If most of them say "no," it is likely a "red light" warning you to stop.

Friend, God is beckoning you into His will and into His plan for your life, and when you step through that door of destiny, you'll leave a black-and-white world and step into a world of full color!

## STUDY QUESTIONS

> Study to shew thyself approved unto God, a workman that needeth not to be ashamed, rightly dividing the word of truth.
> — 2 Timothy 2:15

1.  The number one way God speaks to us and leads us to do His will is through *the voice of the Bible*. The God who is leading you is the same God who inspired the Scriptures, and He will never lead you to do something contradictory to what He has clearly stated in His Word.

    - **Why can you rely on and trust the Bible?**
      *See Matthew 5:18; Luke 21:33; Numbers 23:19; First Kings 8:56; and Isaiah 40:8.*

    - **What is the Word of God useful for?**
      *See Second Timothy 3:15-17; Psalm 119:9,105,130; and Proverbs 4:20-22.*

    - **What can you expect to happen as you read and study Scripture?**
      *See Romans 1:16; Acts 20:32; Hebrews 4:14; and James 1:21.*

2.  In these turbulent, last of the last days, many people — including many Christians — have become very disrespectful of authority, which is something God would never lead us to do. What does the Bible have to say about how we are to treat those in authority? Consider Romans 13:1-7; First Peter 2:13-23; and First Timothy 2:1-4 for some sound advice.

## PRACTICAL APPLICATION

> But be ye doers of the word, and not hearers only, deceiving your own selves.
> —James 1:22

1.  The six specific voices or witnesses that God uses to confirm His direction and will for our lives are *the voice of the Bible, the voice of the Holy Spirit, the voice of your own heart, the voice of spiritual leaders, the voice of circumstances*, and *the voice of faith*. Of these six, what would you say are the top two voices God uses to speak to you most and confirm His leading?

2.  Older, more mature believers who know us well can help us discern the will of God for our life. Who are some of the people God has used through the years to speak into your life? Has God ever used you to speak and confirm His will to someone else? If so, who?

3.  Can you remember a key time when God used a seasoned *spiritual leader* to confirm His leading? If so, what did they speak into your life? How did their words help shape your actions and ultimately impact your life?

TOPIC

# Five Points To Help Keep You On Track

## SCRIPTURES

1.  **Psalm 37:23** — The steps of a good man are ordered by the Lord: and he delighteth in his way.

2.  **Psalm 19:13** — Keep back thy servant also from presumptuous sins; let them not have dominion over me: then shall I be upright, and I shall be innocent from the great transgression.

3.  **Proverbs 29:18** — Where there is no vision, the people perish....

4.  **Habakkuk 2:2** — And the Lord answered me, and said, Write the vision, and make it plain upon tables, that he may run that readeth it.

5.  **Philippians 3:13** — Brethren, I count not myself to have apprehended: but this one thing I do, forgetting those things which are behind, and reaching forth unto those things which are before.

6. **Proverbs 24:3,4** (*TLB*) — Any enterprise is built by wise planning, becomes strong through common sense, and profits wonderfully by keeping abreast of the facts.

7. **Psalm 37:4** — Delight thyself also in the Lord: and he shall give thee the desires of thine heart.

8. **Psalm 20:4** (*NLT*) — May he grant your heart's desires and make all your plans succeed.

9. **1 Corinthians 13:9,12** — For we know in part, and we prophesy in part. For now we see through a glass, darkly; but then face to face: now I know in part; but then shall I know even as also I am known.

10. **Proverbs 3:5,6** — Trust in the Lord with all thine heart; and lean not unto thine own understanding. In all thy ways acknowledge him, and he shall direct thy paths.

## GREEK WORDS

There are no Greek words in this lesson.

## SYNOPSIS

Depending on your age, you may remember when GPS first came out. Initially, in the 1970s it was a system reserved for the military only, but by the mid-80s it was made available to the airline industry and then finally to the public itself around the year 2000. Today, most of us depend on GPS to get us from point A to point B. Whatever it says — turn right, turn left, or make a U-turn — we follow it to a tee.

If we trust a man-made computer program that much, how much more should we trust the Holy Spirit who lives inside us? He is the ultimate GPS who knows everything about everything! He is the Spirit of God Himself who has been to the future and back and knows exactly what paths we need to take each moment of every day in order to fulfill our God-ordained destiny. Are you listening to the Holy Spirit? Are you on track? If you've made mistakes and gotten off course, today is the best day to allow Him to recalculate your journey and do what He tells you to do to get back on track.

**The emphasis of this lesson:**

**If you have gotten off track from what God has told you to do, there are five steps you can take to help get back on track. They are (1) Remember; (2) Review; (3) Report; (4) Recalculate; and (5) Get Back on Track.**

# A Quick Review

As we have noted, Jesus spent a great deal of time talking about the ministry of the Holy Spirit just before laying down His life at Calvary (*see* John 14, 15, and 16). In John 16:13, He specifically said, "Howbeit when he, the Spirit of truth, is come, he will guide you into all truth...." We learned that the word "guide" is the Greek word *hodegos*, which describes *a tour guide — one who shows a traveler the best route to take through unknown country.* Jesus Himself relied on the leading of the Holy Spirit for everything He did, and if we will let Him, the Holy Spirit will show us the safest, fastest, and most pleasurable route to take.

In our second lesson, we focused on Paul's words in Romans 8:14, which says, "For as many as are led by the Spirit of God, they are the sons of God." If you are God's child, you have a right to be led — and should expect to be led — by the Holy Spirit. Don't make the mistake of arrogantly thinking you know more than God and can find your own way through life. Instead, pray like David prayed, "Keep back thy servant also from presumptuous sins; let them not have dominion over me: then shall I be upright, and I shall be innocent from the great transgression" (Psalm 19:13).

Then in our third lesson, we learned that God confirms His direction and will for our lives through six specific voices. They are *the voice of the Bible, the voice of the Holy Spirit, the voice of your own heart, the voice of spiritual leaders, the voice of circumstances,* and *the voice of faith.* Each of these voices act as a witness to the true leading of the Holy Spirit, and as Second Corinthians 13:1 says, "...In the mouth of two or three witnesses shall every word be established."

When there are multiple witnesses confirming something in your life, it is like a *green light* signaling you to move forward. If there are conflicting signs, it is like a *yellow light* telling you to slow down and proceed with caution. And if you sense that several voices are saying, "No, don't do this," you need to take it as a *red light* and go no further.

To help you evaluate where you are and what you need to do to get back on track with what the Holy Spirit is leading you to do, here are five important points to always keep in mind.

# 1. REMEMBER

The first step to confirming you are where God wants you to be is **REMEMBER**, which means to go back to the original leading that He gave you. Clarify in your heart and mind what you believe the Holy Spirit was leading you to do. Having this understanding in front of you is very important. Proverbs 29:18 confirms this saying, "Where there is no vision, the people perish...." When you stray from where God was leading you, it causes you to wander aimlessly. That's why it's vital to regularly remember and reflect on what God first put in your heart.

In Habakkuk 2:2, God tells us, "...Write the vision, and make it plain upon tables, that he may run that readeth it." Whenever you feel like the Holy Spirit has spoken something to you, write it down. As a wise man once said, the shortest pencil is better than the longest memory. When we write things down, it helps to reveal any gaps in our understanding. In some cases, having someone else read the vision to see if they grasp it is also helpful. If you can't read it and run with it, you need to pause and pray, asking God for clarification. The Bible says, "If any of you lacks wisdom, you should ask God, who gives generously to all without finding fault, and it will be given to you" (James 1:5 *NIV*).

Have you stayed in line with the original leading God gave you? Have you deviated from that plan to go another direction? If you sense that you've gotten off track, go back to the original leading God gave you. Ask Him to refresh your memory of what He said, and with His leading clearly before you, you are ready for the second step.

# 2. REVIEW

The next thing you need to do is **REVIEW**, which means taking a thoughtful look at where you are and how you got there. This will help you determine how far off track you are and what you need to do to get back to where you're supposed to be. Although this can sometimes be a very painful process, it's necessary to recalculate and get back on track.

Even the apostle Paul took time to review the facts of where he was in what God led him to do. After accessing his own situation, he wrote,

"Brethren, I count not myself to have apprehended…" (Philippians 3:13). When he says "I count not," it is from the Greek word *logidzomai*, which means *to mathematically count, calculate, tabulate or to make a conclusion.* Historically, this word was used in the bookkeeping world to portray the idea of *a balance sheet* or *a profit-and-loss statement* that a bookkeeper prepared at the end of the month or year.

The use of this word *logidzomai* tells us that Paul was imagining a balance sheet in front of him, and on one side of the page he saw all the things he had accomplished and on the other side he saw all the things he still needed to do. When he did his review, he came to the conclusion that in light of the original leading that God gave him, he had actually not accomplished what he had been called to do.

It's wise to review your current status as well as your progress to see if you're getting where you're supposed to be. A review helps you see if you're on track or falling behind in the leading God gave you for your family, your personal goals, your ministry, or your dream. Scripture tells us, "Any enterprise is built by wise planning, becomes strong through common sense, and profits wonderfully by keeping abreast of the facts" (Proverbs 24:3,4 *TLB*).

Staying ignorant of the facts is the fastest way to get off track. But when you keep abreast of the facts, you profit wonderfully and know exactly where you are in terms of progress.

# 3. REPORT

Once you've reviewed the facts, you need to make an honest analysis — or **REPORT** — of your situation. This report about where you are in light of what God originally led you to do is for you and for those you are close to who need to be informed. This may include your spouse, closest friend, and possibly top team members.

Once you've shared the report, stop and talk about it with those to whom you shared it. This brings the truth of reality to the forefront where it cannot be ignored or denied. Once everything is out in the open for all to see, you must make a choice: Do you sweep the harsh reality of where you're off track under the carpet and pretend everything is all right (when it's not)? Or do you make the decision to embrace the necessary changes to be what God wants you to be and to get back on track again?

Please realize if you're going in the wrong direction, you're never going to reach your destination. The only way to get back on track is to admit you've not been doing what God told you to do and repent for any deviation from His original leading. Then take the necessary steps to return to what God first told you to do.

If you sense the Lord leading you to make a revision or to sharpen your understanding in a way that changes your outlook, then it's time for you to revise your plan.

# 4. RE-CALCULATE AND REVISE

Rick shared how on more than one occasion, he thought he understood what the Lord wanted him to do, only to find out later that he was wrong or simply misunderstood what God had put in his heart. In situations like these, it's better to admit that we're wrong and get back in the flow with what God's Spirit wants us to do rather than to proceed endlessly with something we know isn't exactly His will.

The truth is everyone makes mistakes at times, and the apostle Paul lets us in on a major reason this takes place. He wrote, "For we know in part, and we prophesy in part. For now we see through a glass, darkly; but then face to face: now I know in part; but then shall I know even as also I am known" (1 Corinthians 13:9,12).

In this verse, the word "glass" in Greek refers to *Roman glass* or *a Roman mirror*. Although Roman glass was real glass, it was very opaque and hard to see through. Although you could observe bursts of light coming through, you couldn't clearly see the image on the other side. Similarly, a Roman mirror was very different from today's mirrors. It was actually made out of highly polished metal, and while one could see a little bit of his or her image reflected in it, it wasn't very clear.

So when the apostle Paul says, "For we know in part, and we prophesy in part. For now we see through a glass darkly..." (1 Corinthians 13:9,12), it is the equivalent of him saying, "Right now we can only see some bursts of light and have an idea of what we're supposed to do. Although we can make out part of what we're trying to see and understand, things are just not very clear, and that won't change until we're in eternity."

Our understanding is not as clear today as it will be when we see Jesus face-to-face. Until that time, we will occasionally make mistakes and do things that aren't entirely correct simply because we're not able to see the full picture at the moment. If God has helped you better understand the leading you received from the Holy Spirit, it's time to **RECALCULATE AND REVISE** your plan.

Don't berate yourself if you've made mistakes, and don't waste time wallowing in regret or remorse over it. And by all means, don't stick with the old wrong plan just because you're too embarrassed or proud to say you messed up. That's foolish! Simply repent for any deviation from God's original leading and return to what He first told you to do.

Then, once that recalculation is understood by everyone involved...

# 5. GET BACK ON TRACK

This is where the rubber meets the road. Saying you want to get on track and actually doing it are two different things. In many cases, the spirit is willing but the flesh is weak! The fact is getting back on track may require change. In addition to humbling yourself and admitting you were wrong about some things, you may also have to restructure your financial priorities, reorganize personal assignments, reprioritize your relationships, and reorder your time management.

Through it all, the timeless advice of **Proverbs 3:5 and 6** remains as one of God's greatest promises:

> **Trust in the Lord with all thine heart; and lean not unto thine own understanding.**
>
> **In all thy ways acknowledge him, and he shall direct thy paths.**

Rest assured, when you put your trust in the Lord and reject the pride of thinking you can figure things out on your own, He will direct your life. In fact, Psalm 37:23 says, "The steps of a good man are ordered by the Lord: and he delighteth in his way." As a child of God, you are good and declared righteous in Jesus (*see* 2 Corinthians 5:21). Therefore, you can claim this promise that God is ordering your steps.

Friend, if you feel that you've gotten off track, don't beat yourself up over it. Just be willing to acknowledge that you're off course and accept God's correction. Ask Him to show you where you went wrong and be willing to embrace whatever changes you have to make to get back on track. Again, the five steps to help you evaluate where you are and what you need to do to get back on track with what the Holy Spirit is leading you to do are: *Remember, Review, Report, Recalculate and Revise,* and *Get Back on Track.*

In our final lesson, we will look at more practical, relevant help to help place you back in sync with God's purpose and plan for your life.

## STUDY QUESTIONS

**Study to shew thyself approved unto God, a workman that needeth not to be ashamed, rightly dividing the word of truth.**
**— 2 Timothy 2:15**

1. Our understanding is not as clear today as it will be when we see Jesus face-to-face (*see* 1 Corinthians 13:9,12). Until that time, we will occasionally make mistakes and do things that aren't entirely correct simply because we're not able to see the full picture at the moment. How does this biblical truth help promote peace and alleviate pressure from your life?

2. Trying to figure everything out in your life is both overwhelming and exhausting. The good news is you don't have to! God has a proven remedy for this fruitless tendency and it is found in **Proverbs 3:5-8**. Look up these timeless words of wisdom in a few different Bible versions, and write out the version that comes alive in your heart.

## PRACTICAL APPLICATION

**But be ye doers of the word, and not hearers only, deceiving your own selves.**
**—James 1:22**

1. The first step to confirming you are where God wants you to be is to **Remember,** which means to go back to the original leading that He gave you. Can you remember what the Holy Spirit first called you to do? Did you complete what He asked? If you did, what is the most recent assignment He has given you? Are you still on track to fulfilling it?

2. After you *Remember* what God originally led you to do, the next step is to **Review,** which means taking a thoughtful look at where you are and how you got there. Be honest with yourself and God: Where are you right now in light of what God asked you to do? How much progress have you made toward accomplishing the assignments He's given you?

3.  Make a written **Report** of your *Review* and share it with those you're close to who need to be informed (your spouse, closest friend, top team members). What kind of feedback are they offering? What do you need to **Recalculate and Revise**?

4.  Have you stayed in line with the original leading God gave you? Or have you deviated from that plan to go another direction? If you've not been doing what God asked you to do, admit it, and repent for any deviation from His original leading.

## LESSON 5

TOPIC

# Practical Help in Re-Calculating To Get Back On Track

## SCRIPTURES

1.  **Proverbs 3:5,6** — Trust in the Lord with all thine heart; and lean not unto thine own understanding. In all thy ways acknowledge him, and he shall direct thy paths.

2.  **Psalm 19:13** — Keep back thy servant also from presumptuous sins; let them not have dominion over me: then shall I be upright, and I shall be innocent from the great transgression.

3.  **Proverbs 24:3,4** (*TLB*) — Any enterprise is built by wise planning, becomes strong through common sense, and profits wonderfully by keeping abreast of the facts.

4.  **1 Corinthians 13:9,12** — For we know in part, and we prophesy in part.... For now we see through a glass, darkly; but then face to face: now I know in part; but then shall I know even as also I am known.

5.  **Proverbs 12:15** — The way of a fool is right in his own eyes: but he that hearkeneth unto counsel is wise.

6.  **Proverbs 28:26** — He that trusteth in his own heart is a fool: but whoso walketh wisely, he shall be delivered.

7.  **Proverbs 20:18** — Every purpose is established by counsel: and with good advice make war.

8. **Proverbs 24:6** — For by wise counsel thou shalt make thy war: and in multitude of counsellers there is safety.

9. **Matthew 7:7,8** — Ask, and it shall be given you; seek, and ye shall find; knock, and it shall be opened unto you: for every one that asketh receiveth; and he that seeketh findeth; and to him that knocketh it shall be opened.

10. **James 5:16** — Confess your faults one to another, and pray one for another, that ye may be healed....

11. **Psalm 73:24** — Thou shalt guide me with thy counsel, and afterward receive me to glory.

12. **Proverbs 11:14** — Where no counsel is, the people fall: but in the multitude of counsellers there is safety.

13. **Proverbs 15:22** — Without counsel purposes are disappointed: but in the multitude of counsellers they are established.

14. **Proverbs 19:20** — Hear counsel, and receive instruction, that thou mayest be wise in thy latter end.

15. **Isaiah 41:10** — Fear thou not; for I am with thee: be not dismayed; for I am thy God: I will strengthen thee; yea, I will help thee; yea, I will uphold thee with the right hand of my righteousness.

16. **Psalm 54:4** — Behold, God is mine helper: the Lord is with them that uphold [strengthen] my soul.

17. **Ecclesiastes 4:9,10** — Two are better than one; because they have a good reward for their labour. For if they fall, the one will lift up his fellow: but woe to him that is alone when he falleth; for he hath not another to help him up.

18. **Hebrews 13:17** — Obey them that have the rule over you, and submit yourselves: for they watch for your souls, as they that must give account, that they may do it with joy, and not with grief: for that is unprofitable for you.

19. **Proverbs 4:25-27** — Let thine eyes look right on, and let thine eyelids look straight before thee. Ponder the path of thy feet, and let all thy ways be established. Turn not to the right hand nor to the left: remove thy foot from evil.

20. **Joshua 1:7-9** — Only be thou strong and very courageous, that thou mayest observe to do according to all the law, which Moses my servant commanded thee: turn not from it to the right hand or to the left, that thou mayest prosper whithersoever thou goest. This book

of the law shall not depart out of thy mouth; but thou shalt meditate therein day and night, that thou mayest observe to do according to all that is written therein: for then thou shalt make thy way prosperous, and then thou shalt have good success. Have not I commanded thee? Be strong and of a good courage; be not afraid, neither be thou dismayed: for the Lord thy God is with thee whithersoever thou goest.

## GREEK WORDS

1. "confess" — εξομολογέω (*exomologeo*): a word that means to say out loud, to divulge, or to blurt

2. "faults" — to fall short; to miss the mark; one who misses the mark and falls short of what God expects and approves

3. "one to another" — ἀλλήλων (*allelon*): each other; reciprocally; to each other

4. "that" — ὅπως (*hopos*): so that

5. "healed" — ἰάομαι (*iaomai*): denoted healing that came to pass over a period of time

## SYNOPSIS

The moment you said yes to Jesus and repented of your sins, His Spirit came to live inside you. Instantly, you became the temple of the Holy Spirit (*see* 1 Corinthians 6:19), and in addition to becoming your fulltime teacher, He also took on the role of your supernatural GPS. He stands ready at every moment of every day to lead and guide you in the way you need to go to fulfill your God-given destiny. When you mess up and get off track, He will recalculate and tell you what you need to do to get back on track with God's plan.

**The emphasis of this lesson:**

**The four practical steps to help you get back on course if you've lost your way include: (1) Admit you're off course; (2) Ask for help if you can't get back on course by yourself; (3) Submit to the counsel of those you trust; and (4) Stay steady and don't let anything get you off track again.**

## A Final Review

**The Holy Spirit is your "Guide."** In John 16:13, Jesus declared, "Howbeit when he, the Spirit of truth, is come, he will guide you into all truth...."

We've seen that the word "guide" is the Greek word *hodegos*, which is taken from the word *hodas*, the term for a *road*. When *hodas* becomes *hodegos*, it describes *a tour guide — one who knows all the roads*. As your guide, the Holy Spirit knows the safest, fastest, and most pleasurable route to take. He will even help you avoid the ambushes of the enemy.

What's interesting about this word *hodegos* — translated here as "guide" — is it's the same word used to describe *a guide for the blind*. If someone was blind, they had to put all their trust in their guide to lead them safely and correctly to where they needed to go. By using this word, Jesus is saying, "Let the Holy Spirit be your eyes. Trust Him. He is the Spirit of truth and is able to see what you can't see. He will never lead you astray."

**You can be "led" by the Holy Spirit.** In Romans 8:14, Paul writes, "For as many as are led by the Spirit of God, they are the sons of God." The original Greek text of this verse actually says, "For as many as by the Spirit of God are being led, they are the sons of God." It places the Holy Spirit out in front and us tagging along behind Him, which is a good illustration of the word "led," the Greek word *ago*.

This agricultural term depicted animals led by a rope tied around their necks that followed wherever their owner led them. The owner would "tug" or "pull" the rope, and the animal followed. Hence, the word *ago* indicates *being led by a gentle tug or pull*. Very often the leading of the Holy Spirit is a gentle tug or pull, and we must learn to become sensitive and responsive to His gentle ways.

What's interesting is that the word *ago* — translated here as "led" — also forms the root of the Greek word *agon*, which describes *an intense conflict*, such as a struggle in a wrestling match. Here it depicts *the struggle of the human will*, indicating that sometimes when the Holy Spirit is trying to lead us, our will fights against Him. In those moments, it is like we're thrown into a wrestling match in which our mind struggles against what we know in our heart the Lord is telling us to do. At those times, we must choose to listen to our heart and resist giving in to mental reasoning.

**There are six voices God uses to lead you.** He will speak to you through *the voice of the Bible, the voice of the Holy Spirit, the voice of your own heart, the voice of spiritual leaders, the voice of circumstances*, and *the voice of faith*. Each of these act as a "witness" to the true leading of the Holy Spirit, and as Second Corinthians 13:1 says, "…In the mouth of two or three witnesses shall every word be established."

If all of these witnesses say *yes*, you have a "green light" or a confirmation from God to move forward. If several of these voices say "no," you need to slow down and proceed with caution. If many of them say "no," it is likely a "red light" warning you to stop. When you are seeking God's will in any area of your life, He will use a combination of these six voices to speak to you and can confirm if you are aligned with His will or not.

**There are five steps to help you evaluate where you are and get back on track.** First, you are to *Remember*, which means go back to the original leading the Holy Spirit gave you. Second, *Review*, which means taking a thoughtful look at where you are and how you got there. Third, make an honest *Report* of your situation in light of what God originally led you to do. Once God has helped you better understand His original leading, it's time to *Recalculate and Revise* your plan. The fifth step is to *Get Back on Track*.

# Trust in the Lord
# and Guard Against Presumptuous Sins

One of the greatest promises in Scripture regarding being led by God was penned by King Solomon. Under the inspiration of the Holy Spirit, he wrote:

> **Trust in the Lord with all thine heart; and lean not unto thine own understanding.**
> **In all thy ways acknowledge him, and he shall direct thy paths.**
> **— Proverbs 3:5,6**

Trust in God is developed over time as we choose to trust Him and be confident in His Word instead of trusting in what we think or feel or see. The more we learn to lean on Him and believe what He said in His Word, the more He will direct our path.

Oftentimes we make mistakes and get off track because we act presumptuously. A presumptuous sin is when we act without praying and receiving the leading of the Holy Spirit. We assume in our mind that we are heading in the right direction, but we fail to get God's input. To avoid this fleshly tendency, we have to pray Psalm 19:13, which says, "Keep back thy servant also from presumptuous sins; let them not have dominion over me...."

If you have made mistakes and now find yourself in a mess, don't panic or feel condemned. There is a way to turn things around, and it involves these four simple steps:

1. Admit you're off course.
2. If you can't get back on-course by yourself, ask for help.
3. Submit to the counsel of those you trust.
4. Stay steady and don't let anything get you off track again.

# FOUR PRACTICAL STEPS TO GET BACK ON COURSE

## Step 1: Admit You're Off Course

In order for you to realize and admit you are not where God wants you to be, you have to walk out the five points we covered in Lesson 4. Once more, these include:

1. **Remember** – go back to the original leading the Holy Spirit gave you.
2. **Review** – take a thoughtful look at where you are and how you got there.
3. **Report** – make an honest, written analysis of your situation and share it with those close to you.
4. **Recalculate and Revise** your plan once God helps you see where and how you got off track.
5. **Get Back on Track** – actually taking the steps you need to take to do what God asked.

The Bible says, "Any enterprise is built by wise planning, becomes strong through common sense, and profits wonderfully by keeping abreast of the facts" (Proverbs 24:3,4 *TLB*). Facts are very important because they do not lie. When you stay informed of the facts of where you are and how much progress you've made, you can determine if you're actually doing what the Holy Spirit told you to do.

Everyone makes mistakes — even the most seasoned Christians. And it's foolish to keep going in the wrong direction because you're too embarrassed to admit that you messed up. Rather than waste more time, money, talent, and energy, simply admit you're off course and seek the Holy Spirit to know what you need to do to get back on track.

**Our spiritual vision is limited**. Remember what we learned from the apostle Paul in First Corinthians 13:9 and 12: "For we know in part, and we prophesy in part. For now we see through a glass, darkly; but then face to face: now I know in part; but then shall I know even as also I am known."

We saw that the word "glass" in Greek can refer to *Roman glass* or *a Roman mirror*. Although Roman glass was real glass, it was very cloudy and hard to see through. Only bursts of light could be visibly seen coming through; the image on the other side of the glass was blurry. Similarly, a Roman mirror was made out of highly polished metal, and while one could see a little bit of his or her image reflected in it, it wasn't very clear.

Paul's use of this analogy in First Corinthians 13:9 and 12 is the equivalent of him saying, "Right now we can only see bursts of revelation and direction; the blueprint of God's will for our life is blurry. Although we have an idea of what we're supposed to do, our understanding is not crystal clear. But one day, when we see Jesus face-to-face, we will know everything."

On this side of Heaven, we will occasionally make mistakes because we are humans who don't see things correctly. Once you realize you're off track, repent for any ways you may have deviated from God's plan and return to what He first told you to do. Don't waste time drowning in regret or remorse for your mistakes. If God has helped you better understand the assignment you received from heaven, you're free to start again and revise the way you're carrying it out.

**Walk wisely, not foolishly.** The Bible says, "The way of a fool is right in his own eyes: but he that hearkeneth unto counsel is wise" (Proverbs 12:15). The Word also tells us, "He that trusteth in his own heart is a fool: but whoso walketh wisely, he shall be delivered" (Proverbs 28:26). Friend, don't take the way of a fool. Look for and listen to the counsel of wise, godly people — people who have walked the path you're on and have learned from their mistakes. Hearing and heeding their words of wisdom will help you get back on track.

# Step 2: If You Can't Get Back On Course by Yourself, Then Ask for Help

In some cases, getting back on track is too difficult to accomplish on our own. If that describes where you are, don't be afraid to ask for help. In the same way, don't let pride keep you from reaching out to others who have the answers and resources you need to get back to God's assignment for your life.

Receiving godly counsel is priceless. Proverbs 20:18 says, "Every purpose is established by counsel: and with good advice make war," and Proverbs 24:6 tells us, "For by wise counsel thou shalt make thy war: and in multitude of counsellors there is safety." The fact is all of us have blind spots. Just like when we're driving in a car and there are certain areas we can't see, there are things around us on the road of life that we need help to see. If we are open and humble enough to ask for input from others, we can avoid many crashes.

The question is are you asking for help? Jesus said, "Ask, and it shall be given you; seek, and ye shall find; knock, and it shall be opened unto you: for every one that asketh receiveth; and he that seeketh findeth; and to him that knocketh it shall be opened" (Matthew 7:7,8). If you have a heart to receive help and wise counsel, God will give it to you.

**We need to be honest with others.** A major key to being healed and restored is found in James 5:16, which says, "Confess your faults one to another, and pray one for another, that ye may be healed...." The word "confess" in this verse is the Greek word *exomologeo*, which means *to say out loud*, *to divulge*, or *to blurt*. When you've made a mistake, it is important to share it with a trusted friend or two.

According to this verse, healing is released when you verbalize your "faults." In Greek, the word "faults" means *to fall short* or *to miss the mark*. It depicts *one who misses the mark and falls short of what God expects and approves*. In other words, it denotes *one who has gotten off track*. The Bible says we are to confess these things "one to another," which means *to each other* or *reciprocally*. Why? It is so that we can pray for one another and be "healed." This word "healed" is a translation of the Greek word *iaomai*, which denotes *healing that comes to pass over a period of time*. Essentially, what this is telling us is that if we will admit out loud to those who love us that we've made a mistake, God will begin the process of healing us and getting us back on track.

## Step 3: Submit to the Counsel of Those You Trust

The third step to getting back on track is *submitting to the counsel of those you trust*. The Bible has much to say on the value and need for good, godly counsel. These verses are a great example:

**Thou shalt guide me with thy counsel, and afterward receive me to glory.**

**— Psalm 73:24**

**Where no counsel is, the people fall: but in the multitude of counsellors there is safety.**

**— Proverbs 11:14**

**Without counsel purposes are disappointed: but in the multitude of counsellors they are established.**

**— Proverbs 15:22**

**Hear counsel, and receive instruction, that thou mayest be wise in thy latter end.**

**— Proverbs 19:20**

All these verses tell us that when we seek and receive wise counsel from others, our plans will be firmly established, we'll be kept safe, and we'll make it through this life and into the next one where we'll spend eternity in Heaven with Jesus.

In Isaiah 41:10, God Himself has said, "Fear thou not; for I am with thee: be not dismayed; for I am thy God: I will strengthen thee; yea, I will help thee; yea, I will uphold thee with the right hand of my righteousness." Wow! What a powerful promise!

In Psalm 54:4, David declared, "Behold, God is mine helper: the Lord is with them that uphold [strengthen] my soul." In the midst of extreme difficulty, when King Saul was hunting him down to kill him, David praised God for being his Helper and surrounding him with others who strengthened him. In the same way, God will put people in your life who are filled with wisdom, and if you'll listen, they will speak into your life exactly what you need to hear at the right time.

**We all need healthy relationships.** It has been said that no man is an island unto himself, and it's true. We are simply not made to do life alone. Ecclesiastes 4:9 and 10 confirm this by saying, "Two are better than one; because they have a good reward for their labour. For if they fall, the one will lift up his fellow: but woe to him that is alone when he falleth; for he hath not another to help him up." There will be times in each of our lives when we will run off course and end up in a ditch. It's on those occasions that we really come to understand the blessing of having others in our lives.

We need friends on our level as well as healthy, godly leaders we are submitted to. Hebrews 13:17 tells us, "Obey them that have the rule over you, and submit yourselves: for they watch for your souls…." Your pastor and the leaders in your church have been entrusted by God with the responsibility to watch over your spiritual health and development. Rather than having a frustrated attitude and resisting their input, God wants you to submit to their leadership. Good leaders love you and want what's best for you. When you're willing to listen, their words of wisdom can help you recover from setbacks and recalculate your course so you can get back on track.

## Step 4: Stay Steady and Don't Let Anything Get You Off Track Again

Once you listen to the wise counsel God has given you and you get back on track, make it your aim to stay the course and resist distractions. This principle is seen clearly in Proverbs 4:25-27, which says, "Let thine eyes look right on, and let thine eyelids look straight before thee. Ponder the path of thy feet, and let all thy ways be established. Turn not to the right hand nor to the left: remove thy foot from evil."

God doesn't want us wandering aimlessly, distracted, or bouncing from one thing to another. Although there are many things we could be doing, He wants us focused on what He has asked us to do. If we're not careful, doing something good can rob us of the opportunity to do what is best. This is why periodically walking through the five steps outlined in Lesson 4 are so vital. It helps us to discern if we're still on track with what God asked us to do, and if we're not, it helps us adjust our course.

Look at what God told Joshua when he received the mantle of leadership over the nation of Israel:

> **Only be thou strong and very courageous, that thou mayest observe to do according to all the law, which Moses my servant commanded thee: turn not from it to the right hand or to the left, that thou mayest prosper whithersoever thou goest.**
> **— Joshua 1:7**

Are you seeing the recurring theme? God's words to Joshua and the instruction of Proverbs 4:25-27 basically say, "Keep your eyes focused on what I told you [My Word]; don't deviate to the right or the left of it. If you stay the course, you will succeed."

How important is keeping God's Word in front of you? We find the answer in the next verse where God tells Joshua:

> **This book of the law shall not depart out of thy mouth; but thou shalt meditate therein day and night, that thou mayest observe to do according to all that is written therein: for then thou shalt make thy way prosperous, and then thou shalt have good success.**
>
> **— Joshua 1:8**

In addition to staying in the Word, we need to keep the specific assignment the Holy Spirit has given us right in front of us. That's what God meant when He told Habakkuk to "…Write the vision, and make it plain upon tables, that he may run that readeth it" (Habakkuk 2:2).

Friend, it takes strength and courage to stay the course and do the will of God. As you're running your race and doing all God has called you to do, there will sometimes be opportunities to be discouraged, afraid, and dismayed by what you see, what you hear, and how you feel. That is what Joshua faced, which is why God told Him — and He is telling us — these powerful words:

> **Have not I commanded thee? Be strong and of a good courage; be not afraid, neither be thou dismayed: for the Lord thy God is with thee whithersoever thou goest.**
>
> **— Joshua 1:9**

The greatest source of strength, courage, and peace is in knowing that **GOD IS WITH YOU WHEREVER YOU GO!** He will never leave you or forsake you. He always has your best interest at heart, and when you trust in Him with all your heart instead of leaning on your own understanding, He will direct your path. Friend, if you've gotten off track, it's time to fess up and admit you messed up. God will help you get back on track every time you surrender to Him and follow His leading.

## STUDY QUESTIONS

> **Study to shew thyself approved unto God, a workman that needeth not to be ashamed, rightly dividing the word of truth.**
> **— 2 Timothy 2:15**

1. Strengthening your relationship with the Holy Spirit by investing time in God's Word and in prayer is one of the best ways to fine-tune your ears to hear His voice. According to these verses, what can you expect the Spirit to do in your life?

   - **Psalm 25:9,12-14**
   - **Psalm 32:8; Isaiah 30:21**
   - **Matthew 10:19,20; Luke 12:11,12**
   - **John 10:27; 14:16,26; 16:13**
   - **2 Timothy 4:17**

2. Take a few moments to carefully read Ecclesiastes 4:8-12 along with Proverbs 17:17 and 27:17. What is the Holy Spirit showing you about the value of friendships in your life?

3. We've talked a lot about the importance of having godly friends to help us see and deal with our own mistakes — we see this all over Scripture. Who did David have in his life to help him confront and find freedom from secret sin? How did he help David see the truth about his situation? (*See* 2 Samuel 11; 12:1-23.) And what did David do to get back on track? (*See* Psalm 32:1-7; 51.)

## PRACTICAL APPLICATION

> But be ye doers of the word, and not hearers only,
> deceiving your own selves.
> —James 1:22

1. What is your normal response once you realize you've messed up and gotten off track? Do you tend to ignore, justify, or hide your actions? Or do you examine your motives, admit where you were wrong, and begin to work to make things right?

2. Do you follow God's instruction in James 5:16 and "confess" your faults and mistakes to someone you trust? If not, what is keeping you from doing so? Is there anyone in your life that you trust and feel safe enough with to have this kind of conversation? If you don't have someone, pray and ask God to connect you with the right peers and mentors to do life with.

# Notes

# CLAIM YOUR FREE RESOURCE!

As a way of introducing you further to the teaching ministry of Rick Renner, we would like to send you free of charge his teaching CD, "How To Receive a Miraculous Touch From God."

In His earthly ministry, Jesus commonly healed *all* who were sick of *all* their diseases. In this profound message, learn about the manifold dimensions of Christ's wisdom, goodness, power, and love toward all humanity who came to Him in faith with their needs.

☑ **YES, I want to receive Rick Renner's monthly teaching letter!**

Simply scan the QR code to claim this resource or go to: **renner.org/claim-your-free-offer**

WITH US!